W9-CFK-975

A Beginning-to-Read Book

Spring

by Mary Lindeen

NORWOOD HOUSE PRESS

DEAR CAREGIVER, The *Beginning to Read—Read and Discover* books provide emergent readers the opportunity to explore the world through nonfiction while building early reading skills. The text integrates both common sight words and content vocabulary. These key words are featured on lists provided at the back of the book to help your child expand his or her sight word recognition, which helps build reading fluency. The content words expand vocabulary and support comprehension.

Nonfiction text is any text that is factual. The Common Core State Standards call for an increase in the amount of informational text reading among students. The Standards aim to promote college and career readiness among students. Preparation for college and career endeavors requires proficiency in reading complex informational texts in a variety of content areas. You can help your child build a foundation by introducing nonfiction early. To further support the CCSS, you will find Reading Reinforcement activities at the back of the book that are aligned to these Standards.

Above all, the most important part of the reading experience is to have fun and enjoy it!

Sincerely,

Shannon Cannon

Shannon Cannon, Ph.D.
Literacy Consultant

Norwood House Press • P.O. Box 316598 • Chicago, Illinois 60631
For more information about Norwood House Press please visit our website at
www.norwoodhousepress.com or call 866-565-2900.
© 2016 Norwood House Press. Beginning-to-Read™ is a trademark of Norwood House Press.
All rights reserved. No part of this book may be reproduced or utilized in any form or by any
means without written permission from the publisher.

Editor: Judy Kentor Schmauss
Designer: Lindaanne Donohoe

Photo Credits:
Shutterstock, cover, 1, 6, 10-11, 12-13, 14-15, 16, 17, 18-19, 20-21, 22-23, 24-25, 26-27, 28-29; Dreamstime, 7; Phil Martin, 3, 8-9

Library of Congress Cataloging-in-Publication Data
    Lindeen, Mary, author.
    Spring / by Mary Lindeen.
        pages cm. – (A beginning to read book)
    Summary: "Spring is a special time of year. The weather warms up, snow changes to rain, flowers bloom,
and baby animals are born. Find out how May Day is celebrated and what new things there are to see in
spring. This title includes reading activities and a word list"– Provided by publisher.
    Audience: Grades K to 3.
    ISBN 978-1-59953-679-8 (library edition : alk. paper)
    ISBN 978-1-60357-764-9 (ebook)
    1. Spring–Juvenile literature. I. Title.
    QB637.5.L56 2015
    508.2–dc23

                                   2014047619

Manufactured in the United States of America in Stevens Point, Wisconsin. 275N-062015

It is spring.
Spring comes after winter.

The air gets warm in spring.

The snow melts.

The rain comes.

People get out their umbrellas.
They put on their boots.

You can splash in the puddles!

A rainbow comes
after the rain.

What colors do
you see?

It is windy in the spring.

You can fly a kite!

Plants come up in the spring.

Flowers grow and bloom.

New leaves grow
on the trees.

The grass is green
again.

Farmers plant their crops
in the spring.

The warm sun will help them grow.

Birds that went
away for the
winter come back.

This robin is a
sign that spring
is coming.

Baby animals are born in the spring.

How many baby bunnies can you see?

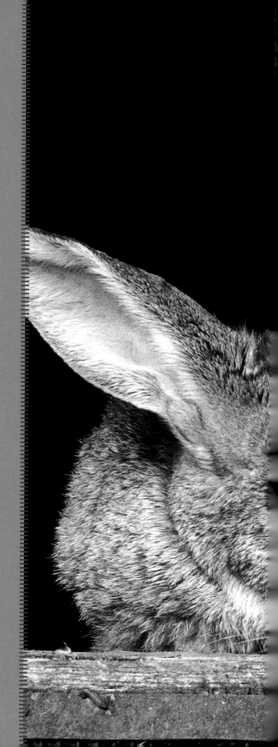

Chicks come out of their eggs.

Little lambs play in the sun.

May Day is in the spring.

Some people give their friends baskets of flowers.

Spring gives us
many new things
to see.

What do you like
to see in spring?

·· **Reading Reinforcement** ··

CRAFT AND STRUCTURE

To check your child's understanding of the book, recreate the following diagram on a sheet of paper. Ask your child to complete the diagram by identifying some of the cause-and-effect relationships in the book:

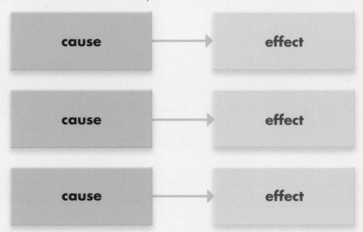

VOCABULARY: Learning Content Words

Content words are words that are specific to a particular topic. All of the content words for this book can be found on page 32. Use some or all of these content words to complete one or more of the following activities:

- Ask your child to sort the content words into two, three, or four categories of their own choosing. Then have him or her explain what the words in each category have in common.

- Help your child look for a smaller word within each content word. Make a list of the content words that have smaller words within them.

- Help your child find pairs of content words that have something in common, either in meaning, structure, or both.

- Have your child find and cut out two magazine pictures that remind him or her of the meaning of each content word.

- Help your child find content words from this book in other written materials in your home.

FOUNDATIONAL SKILLS: Verbs

Verbs are action words. Have your child identify the words that are verbs in the list below. Then help your child find verbs in this book.

melts	umbrellas	grass	eggs	rainbow
splash	fly	come	grow	play

CLOSE READING OF INFORMATIONAL TEXT

Close reading helps children comprehend text. It includes reading a text, discussing it with others, and answering questions about it. Use these questions to discuss this book with your child:

- What season comes before spring?
- Why does the snow melt in the spring?
- What is the reason for planting crops in the spring?
- What do flowers have to do with May Day?
- What would happen if you tried to fly a kite on a day that was not windy?
- Do you like spring? Why or why not?

FLUENCY

Fluency is the ability to read accurately with speed and expression. Help your child practice fluency by using one or more of the following activities:

- Reread this book to your child at least two times while he or she uses a finger to track each word as you read it.
- Read the first sentence aloud. Then have your child reread the sentence with you. Continue until you have finished this book.
- Ask your child to read aloud the words they know on each page of this book. (Your child will learn additional words with subsequent readings.)
- Have your child practice reading this book several times to improve accuracy, rate, and expression.

••• Word List •••

Spring uses the 85 words listed below. *High-frequency* words are those words that are used most often in the English language. They are sometimes referred to as sight words because children need to learn to recognize them automatically when they read. *Content words* are any words specific to a particular topic. Regular practice reading these words will enhance your child's ability to read with greater fluency and comprehension.

High-Frequency Words

a	day	like	see	up
after	do	little	some	us
again	for	many	that	went
air	get(s)	may	the	what
and	give(s)	new	their	will
are	help	of	them	you
away	how	on	they	
back	in	out	things	
can	is	people	this	
come(s, ing)	it	put	to	

Content Words

animals	chicks	grass	play	spring
baby	colors	green	puddles	sun
baskets	crops	grow	rain	trees
birds	eggs	kite	rainbow	umbrellas
bloom	farmers	lambs	robin	warm
boots	flowers	leaves	sign	windy
born	fly	melts	snow	winter
bunnies	friends	plant(s)	splash	

••• **About the Author**

Mary Lindeen is a writer, editor, parent, and former elementary school teacher. She has written more than 100 books for children and edited many more. She specializes in early literacy instruction and books for young readers, especially nonfiction.

••• **About the Advisor**

Dr. Shannon Cannon is a teacher educator in the School of Education at UC Davis, where she also earned her Ph.D. in Language, Literacy, and Culture. She serves on the clinical faculty, supervising pre-service teachers and teaching elementary methods courses in reading, effective teaching, and teacher action research.

W9-DBC-813

Claus Stamm

Three Strong Women

A TALL TALE FROM JAPAN

Pictures by
Jean and Mou-sien Tseng

PUFFIN BOOKS

FRANKLIN PIERCE COLLEGE
LIBRARY
RINDGE, N.H. 03461

PUFFIN BOOKS
Published by the Penguin Group
Penguin Books USA Inc., 375 Hudson Street, New York, New York 10014, U.S.A.
Penguin Books Ltd, 27 Wrights Lane, London W8 T5Z, England
Penguin Books Australia Ltd, Ringwood, Victoria, Australia
Penguin Books Canada Ltd, 10 Alcorn Avenue, Toronto, Ontario, Canada M4V 3B2
Penguin Books (N.Z.) Ltd, 182–190 Wairau Road, Auckland 10, New Zealand

Penguin Books Ltd, Registered Offices: Harmondsworth, Middlesex, England

First published in the United States of America by The Viking Press, 1962
Published with illustrations by Jean and Mou-sien Tseng by Viking Penguin, a division
of Penguin Books USA Inc., 1990
Published in Puffin Books, 1993

1   3   5   7   9   10   8   6   4   2

Copyright © Claus Stamm and Kazue Mizumura, 1962
Copyright renewed Claus Stamm and Kazue Mizumura, 1990
Illustrations copyright © Jean Tseng and Mou-sien Tseng, 1990
All rights reserved

LIBRARY OF CONGRESS CATALOGING-IN-PUBLICATION DATA
Stamm, Claus.
Three strong women / by Claus Stamm and Kazue Mizumura;
illustrated by Jean and Mou-sien Tseng. p.   cm.
"First published in the United States of America by the Viking
Press, 1962; published with illustrations by Viking, a division of
Penguin Books USA Inc., 1990."
—T.p. verso.
Summary: When the famous wrestler Forever Mountain tickles a plump
little girl, the consequence is that he must be trained by her, her
mother, and her grandmother.
ISBN 0-14-054530-1
[1. Fairy tales.   2. Folklore—Japan.]   I. Mizumura, Kazue.
II. Tseng, Jean, ill.   III. Tseng, Mou-Sien, ill.   IV. Title.
[PZ8.S48Th   1993]   398.21—dc20   [E]   92-25331

Printed in the United States of America
Set in Novarese Medium

Except in the United States of America, this book is sold subject
to the condition that it shall not, by way of trade or otherwise,
be lent, re-sold, hired out, or otherwise circulated without the
publisher's prior consent in any form of binding or cover other than
that in which it is published and without a similar condition including
this condition being imposed on the subsequent purchaser.

OVER
PZ
7
.S77
Th
1993

For
Dr. Seiler, Dr. Payson
and
the Beekman Downtown Hospital
in order of their appearance

Long ago, in Japan, there lived a famous wrestler. One day he decided to make his way to the capital city to wrestle before the Emperor.

He strode down the road on legs thick as the trunks of small trees. He had been walking for seven hours and could walk for seven more without getting tired. The time was autumn.

The wrestler hummed to himself, "Zun-zun-zun," in time with the long swing of his legs. Wind blew through his thin brown robe, and he wore no sword at his side. He needed no sword, even in the darkest and loneliest places, and few tailors would have been able to make warm clothes for a man so broad and tall. He felt strong, healthy, and rather conceited.

He thought: "They call me Forever-Mountain because I am a good wrestler. I'm a fine, brave man and far too modest ever to say so. . . ."

Just then he saw a girl who must have come up from the nearby river, for she steadied a bucket on her head. Her hands on the bucket were small, and there was a dimple on each thumb. She was a round little girl with red cheeks and a nose like a friendly button. Her eyes looked as though she were thinking of ten thousand funny stories at once. She clambered up onto the road and walked ahead of the wrestler.

"If I don't tickle that fat girl, I shall regret it all my life," said the wrestler to himself. "She will squeak and I shall laugh and laugh. If she drops her bucket, I can run and fill it again and carry it home for her."

He tiptoed up and poked her lightly in the ribs.

"Kochokochokocho!" he said, a fine, ticklish sound in Japanese.

The girl gave a satisfying squeal, giggled, and brought one arm down so that the wrestler's hand was caught between it and her body.

"Ho-ho-ho! You've caught me! I can't move at all!" said the wrestler.

"I know," said the jolly girl.

He felt that it was very good-tempered of her to take a joke so well, and started to pull his hand free. Somehow, he could not.

He tried again, using a little more strength.

"Now, now—let me go, little girl," he said. "I am a powerful man. If I pull hard I might hurt you."

"Pull," said the girl. "I admire powerful men."

She began to walk, and though the wrestler tugged and pulled until his feet dug great furrows in the ground, he had to follow.

Ten minutes later, still tugging while trudging helplessly after her, he was glad that the road was lonely and no one was there to see.

"Please let me go," he pleaded. "I am the famous wrestler Forever-Mountain. I must go show my strength before the Emperor"—he burst out weeping from shame and confusion—"and you're hurting my hand!"

The girl steadied the bucket on her head with her free hand and dimpled sympathetically over her shoulder. "You poor, sweet little Forever-Mountain," she said. "Are you tired? Shall I carry you?

"I do not want you to carry me. I want you to let me go. I want to forget I ever saw you. What do you want with me?" moaned the pitiful wrestler.

"I only want to help you," said the girl, now pulling him steadily up and up a narrow mountain path. "Oh, I am sure you'll have no more trouble than anyone else against the other wrestlers. You'll win, or else you'll lose, and you won't be too badly hurt either way. But aren't you afraid you might meet a really *strong* man someday?"

Forever-Mountain turned white. He stumbled. He was imagining being laughed at throughout Japan as "Hardly-Ever-Mountain."

She glanced back.

"You see? Tired already," she said. "I'll walk more slowly. Why don't you come along to my mother's house and let us make a strong man of you? The wrestling in the capital won't begin for three months. I know, because Grandmother thought she'd go. You'd be spending all that time in bad company and wasting what little power you have."

"All right. Three months. I'll come," said the wrestler. He felt he had nothing more to lose. Also, he feared that the girl might be angry if he refused, and place him in the top of a tree until he changed his mind.

"Fine," she said happily. "We are almost there."

She freed his hand. It was red and a little swollen. "But if you break your promise and run off, I'll have to chase you and carry you back."

Soon they arrived in a small valley where a simple farmhouse with a thatched roof stood.

"Grandmother is at home, but she is an old lady and she's probably sleeping." The girl shaded her eyes with one hand. "But Mother should be bringing our cow back from the field. There's Mother now!"

She waved. The woman coming around the corner of the house put down the cow she was carrying and waved back.

She smiled and came across the grass, walking with a lively bounce like her daughter's. Well, maybe her bounce was a little more solid, thought the wrestler.

"Excuse me," she said. "These mountain paths are full of stones. They hurt the cow's feet. And who is the nice young man, Maru-me?"

The girl explained. "And we have only three months!" she finished anxiously.

"Well, it's not long enough to do much, but it's not so short a time that we can't do something," said her mother, looking thoughtful. "But he does look terribly feeble. He'll need a lot of good things to eat. Maybe he can help Grandmother with some of the easy housework."

"That will be fine!" said the girl, and she called her grandmother—loudly, for the old lady was a little deaf.

"I'm coming!" came a creaky voice from inside the house, and a little old woman leaning on a stick tottered out of the door. As she came toward them she stumbled over the roots of a great oak tree.

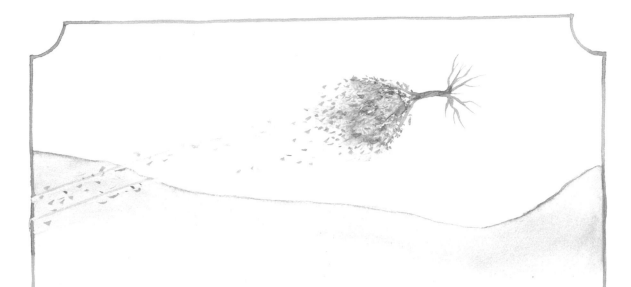

"Heh! My eyes aren't what they used to be. That's the fourth time this month I've stumbled over that tree," she complained and, wrapping her skinny arms about its trunk, pulled it out of the ground.

"Oh, Grandmother! You should have let me pull it up for you," said Maru-me.

"Hm. I hope I didn't hurt my poor old back," muttered the old lady. She called out, "Daughter! Throw that tree away like a good girl, so no one will fall over it. But make sure it doesn't hit anybody."

"You can help Mother with the tree," Maru-me said to Forever-Mountain. "On second thought, you'd better not help. Just watch."

Her mother went to the tree, picked it up in her two hands, and threw it—clumsily and with a little gasp.

Up went the tree, sailing end over end, growing smaller and smaller as it flew. It landed with a faint crash far up the mountainside.

"Ah, how clumsy," she said. "I meant to throw it *over* the mountain. It's probably blocking the path now, and I'll have to move it tomorrow."

The wrestler was not listening. He had very quietly fainted.

"Oh! We must put him to bed," said Maru-me.

"Poor, feeble young man," said her mother.

"I hope we can do something for him. Here, let me carry him, he's light," said the grandmother. She slung him over her shoulder and carried him into the house, creaking along with her cane.

The next day they began the work of making Forever-Mountain over into what they thought a strong man should be. They gave him the simplest food to eat, and the toughest. Day by day they prepared his rice with less and less water, until no ordinary man could have chewed or digested it.

Every day he was made to do the work of five men, and every evening he wrestled with Grandmother. Maru-me and her mother agreed that Grandmother, being old and feeble, was the least likely to injure him accidentally. They hoped the exercise might be good for her rheumatism.

He grew stronger and stronger but was hardly aware of it. Grandmother could still throw him easily into the air—and catch him again—without ever changing her sweet old smile.

He quite forgot that outside this valley he was one of the greatest wrestlers in Japan and was called Forever-Mountain. His legs had been like logs; now they were like pillars. His big hands were hard as stones, and when he cracked his knuckles the sound was like trees splitting on a cold night.

Sometimes he did an exercise that wrestlers do in Japan—raising one foot high above the gound and bringing it down with a crash. Then people in nearby villages looked up at the winter sky and said that it was very late in the year for thunder.

Soon he could pull up a tree as well as the grandmother. He could even throw one—but only a small distance. One evening, near the end of his third month, he wrestled with Grandmother and held her down for half a minute.

"Heh-heh!" She chortled and got up, smiling with every wrinkle. "I'd never have believed it!"

Maru-me squealed with joy and threw her arms around him—gently, for she was afraid of cracking his ribs.

"Very good, very good! What a strong man," said her mother, who had just come home from the fields, carrying, as usual, the cow. She put the cow down and patted the wrestler on the back.

They agreed that he was now ready to show some *real* strength before the Emperor.

"Take the cow along with you tomorrow when you go," said the mother. "Sell her and buy yourself a belt—a silken belt. Buy the fattest and heaviest one you can find. Wear it when you appear before the Emperor, as a souvenir from us."

"I wouldn't think of taking your only cow. You've already done too much for me. And you'll need her to plow the fields, won't you?"

They burst out laughing. Maru-me squealed, her mother roared. The grandmother cackled so hard and long that she choked and had to be pounded on the back.

"Oh, dear," said the mother, still laughing. "You didn't think we used our cow for *work*! Why, Grandmother here is stronger than five cows!"

"The cow is our pet," Maru-me giggled. "She has lovely brown eyes."

"But it really gets tiresome having to carry her back and forth each day so that she has enough grass to eat," said her mother.

"Then you must let me give you all the prize money that I win," said Forever-Mountain.

"Oh, no! We wouldn't think of it!" said Maru-me. "Because we all like you too much to sell you anything. And it is not proper to accept gifts of money from strangers."

"True," said Forever-Mountain. "I will now ask your mother's and grandmother's permission to marry you. I want to be one of the family."

"Oh! I'll make a wedding dress!" said Maru-me.

The mother and grandmother pretended to consider very seriously, but they quickly agreed.

Next morning Forever-Mountain tied his hair up in the topknot that all Japanese wrestlers wear, and got ready to leave. He thanked Maru-me and her mother and bowed very low to the grandmother, since she was the oldest and had been a fine wrestling partner. Then he picked up the cow and trudged up the mountain. When he reached the top, he slung the cow over one shoulder and waved good-bye to Maru-me.

At the first town he came to, Forever-Mountain sold the cow. She brought a good price because she was unusually fat from never having worked in her life. With the money, he bought the heaviest silken belt he could find.

When he reached the palace grounds, many of the other wrestlers were already there, sitting about, eating enormous bowls of rice, comparing one another's weight, and telling stories. They paid little attention to Forever-Mountain, except to wonder why he had arrived so late this year. Some of them noticed that he had grown very quiet and took no part at all in their boasting.

All the ladies and gentlemen of the court were waiting in a special courtyard for the wrestling to begin. They wore many robes, one on top of another, heavy with embroidery and gold cloth, and sweat ran down their faces and froze in the winter afternoon. The gentlemen had long swords so weighted with gold and precious stones that they could never have used them, even if they had known how. The court ladies, with their long black hair hanging down behind, had their faces painted dead white, which made them look frightened. They had pulled out their real eyebrows and painted new ones high above the place where eyebrows are supposed to be, and this made them all look as though they were very surprised at something.

Behind a screen sat the Emperor—by himself, because he was too noble for ordinary people to look at. He was a lonely old man with a kind, tired face. He hoped the wrestling would end quickly so that he could go to his room and write poems.

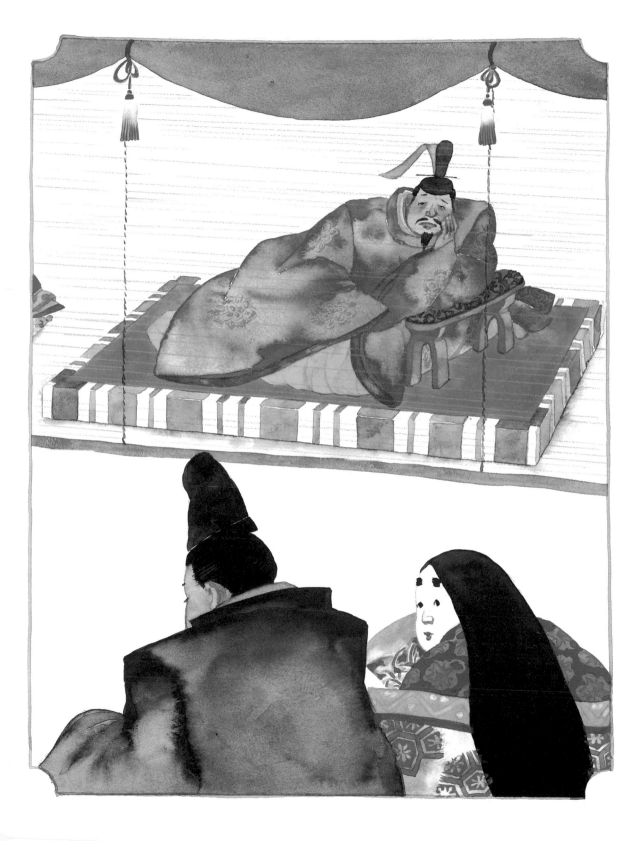

The first two wrestlers chosen to fight were Forever-Mountain and a wrestler who was said to have the biggest stomach in the country. He and Forever-Mountain both threw some salt into the ring. It was said that this drove away evil spirits.

Then the other wrestler, moving his stomach somewhat out of the way, raised his foot and brought it down with a fearful stamp. He glared fiercely at Forever-Mountain as if to say, "Now *you* stamp, you poor frightened man!"

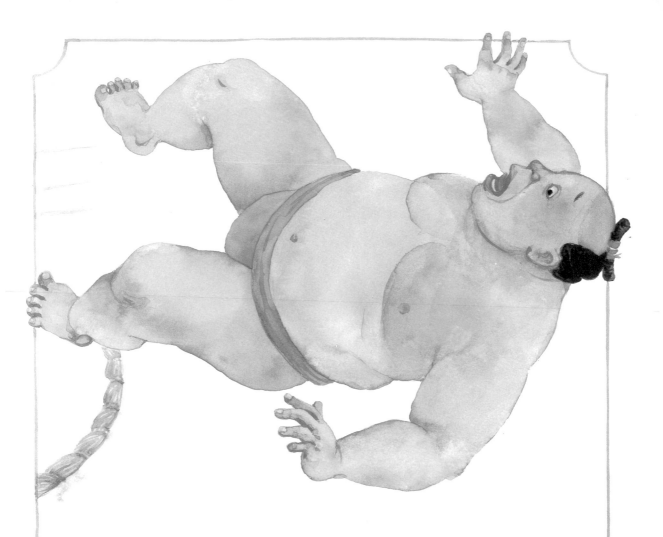

Forever-Mountain raised his foot. He brought it down.

There was a sound like thunder, the earth shook, and the other wrestler bounced into the air and out of the ring, as gracefully as any soap bubble.

He picked himself up and bowed to the Emperor's screen.

"The earth-god is angry. Possibly there is something the matter with the salt," he said. "I do not think I shall wrestle this season." And he walked out, looking very suspiciously over one shoulder at Forever-Mountain.

Five other wrestlers then and there decided that they were not wrestling this season, either.

From then on, Forever-Mountain brought his foot down lightly. As each wrestler came into the ring, he picked him up very gently, carried him out, and placed him before the Emperor's screen, bowing most courteously every time.

The court ladies' eyebrows went up even higher. The gentlemen looked disturbed and a little afraid. They loved to see fierce, strong men tugging and grunting at each other, but Forever-Mountain was a little too much for them. Only the Emperor was happy. With the wrestling over so quickly, he would have that much more time to write his poems. He ordered all the prize money handed over to Forever-Mountain.

"But," he said, "you had better not wrestle any more." He stuck a finger through his screen and waggled it at the other wrestlers, who were sitting on the ground weeping with disappointment like great fat babies.

Forever-Mountain promised not to wrestle any more. Everybody looked relieved. The wrestlers sitting on the ground almost smiled.

"I think I shall become a farmer," Forever-Mountain said.

Maru-me was waiting for him. When she saw him coming, she ran down the mountain, picked him up, together with the heavy bags of prize money, and carried him halfway up the mountainside. Then she giggled and put him down. The rest of the way she let him carry her.

Forever-Mountain kept his promise to the Emperor and never fought in public again. His name was forgotten in the capital. But up in the mountains, sometimes, the earth shakes and rumbles, and they say that it is Forever-Mountain and Maru-me's grandmother practicing wrestling.